Five Truths

For

Single Moms

*Finding the silver lining in every
season of single motherhood*

Johanna Boscarello

ISBN-13: 978-1979416573

ISBN-10: 1979416575

Dedication Page

They say it takes a village, and I absolutely know this to be true. This book is dedicated to our village...to every single person who has been with us along this journey. I know we wouldn't be who or where we are without God and without all of you. I love you all so much and thank you from the bottom of my heart!!

Thank you

I also wanted to say a very special thank you to Michele Abraham and Jelani Pinnock, for the editing and cover creation respectively. Without the both of you, I am not sure this book would have come together. You have been huge blessings to me in this process and I am ever so thankful!! Love you both!!

Five Truths for Single Moms

Table of Contents

Introduction

God led you to pick up this book for a reason. I truly believe that. Just as I believe He gave me the words for this book specifically for YOU. I am not sure what season of life you are in as a single Mom, but I do know it is challenging. Even amidst the challenges, there is hope. Here is something that God has placed on my heart lately, and I want to share it with you as we look at these truths together.

Lately I have been seeing anchors (real ones, not imagined) in different places, or I've heard songs about them. In whatever capacity, they keep popping up. I knew God had a reason for it, so I knew I had to do some research.

Before I had the chance, my older daughter came to me to show me that recently God had been bringing the same verse to her over and over. I told her to get my commentary (book of Bible verse explanations) and we would look it up, and we did. Then I thought of the anchor and decided to look it up with her.

She had known that God had put anchors on my heart because we had painted canvases on the past Sunday and I painted an anchor and told her what it meant to me right now. So then we looked up the Bible verse about hope and anchors. Here is what we found:

Hebrews 6: 19,

We have this hope as an anchor for the soul, firm and secure. It enters the inner sanctuary behind the curtain

I have a study Bible, so we looked at the notes for these verses. What I found brought me so much hope in this world that many times leaves me feeling hopeless. Thank God we can ALWAYS have hope in Jesus. Here is what we found:

Like an anchor holding a ship safely in position, our hope in Christ guarantees our safety.

Let's stop right here and think about this for a second. Like an anchor holds a ship, Christ holds us! It goes on…

Whereas the ship's anchor goes down to the ocean bed, the Christian's anchor goes up into the true, heavenly sanctuary.

Our anchor is in God…and He is our sanctuary. We find our hope in Jesus.

Whatever the circumstance you are going through...our God is bigger. Does that mean it will be easy? No it doesn't. It means that keeping our eyes on the NEVER changing God of Heaven gives us hope.

My prayer for you as you are reading this book is that you will find hope in these pages, and hope in Jesus. As we explore each of the five truths, they will have an accompanying life application chapter. Within the life application will be five tips on how to apply the truth to your life. This is not a fix-all book that will magically make your life perfect. It is a book written with grace and love by someone who has been there and who is still there, and who wants to bring you hope.

In the trenches with you,

~*Johanna*

My Story

So...I finished this book and was not sure what to do with it. A few people asked me if they could read it, and I asked a few people to read it. I was just looking for some feedback and maybe guidance as to what I should do with it. One of those people asked me a question that I felt led to address. She said "What is your story?" So I thought about it for a while and I knew that I needed to share part of my story in order for everyone reading this to know where I am coming from. So here is an abbreviated version of my story...On a side note, I can't tell you my journey as a single Mom without sharing my relationship with Jesus. So....without further ado...my story:

My parents divorced when I was eight and my Mom raised the three of us (my older sister, myself, and my younger brother). We would see my dad, sometimes regularly, sometimes not. We lived in a two bedroom apartment in which my Mom slept on the couch. To be honest, I was pretty oblivious to any struggle back then. For me, it was my normal.

Within the span of a few years when I was a teenager, my Mom was diagnosed with Multiple sclerosis, my grandpa passed away from cancer, my mom got divorced from my step-dad, and my grandma passed away from heart failure. To be honest, I closed myself off...closed my heart off. Worry was my constant companion. Was I good enough? What if someone didn't like me or love me enough? Was something terrible going to happen to someone else I loved?

Then I met this great guy who was my best friend. We got married and things were great...then I miscarried a baby I wanted more than anything. I was devastated. During these many difficult seasons, I would reach out to God and pray, but not often. Then I became pregnant again and gave birth to my beautiful daughter Andrea and my heart overflowed with so much love for this precious little girl. But again, things would not turn out how I wanted, and my marriage ended in divorce. At this time, worry was still my constant companion.

My sister and her children moved in with me at this time because she was a struggling single mom and I was a new single mom to an almost two year old. My sister started going to church every Sunday. She would come home and talk about how the Pastor was funny and how I would like him. She always asked me to go, but I repeatedly told her no. Thank God she kept asking.

The first time I heard Philippians 4:5-6, "Do not be anxious about anything, but in every situation, by prayer and petition, with thanksgiving, present your requests to God. And the peace of God, which transcends all understanding, will guard your hearts and your minds in Christ Jesus." my heart started to open. The worry started to fade. Even today, this is my go to verse when I start to stress or worry.

During this time I met another guy and we dated and married a short time later. Shortly after, I became pregnant with my second daughter, Alexa. I was super excited to be having another girl, but once again, things did not turn out how I expected, and during my pregnancy, this marriage also ended in divorce.

I was continuing to learn more and more about God, and it was towards the end of this second divorce that I gave my heart to Him and asked Him to be my savior. I knew I needed His promises and His love in my life. For too long I had tried to fill the void that was left by so much pain and loss with other things. I tried to be good enough or look a certain way for people to love me. I'm sure you know the song..."Looking for love in all the wrong places" ~ well this was me. No matter how hard or what I tried, nothing ever filled the void. Nothing that is, until Jesus.

Fast forward to today. I have been a single Mom for about twelve years. In that time, I have been fortunate to have the love and support of my family. My Mom has always been my biggest cheerleader, and it was from her I learned to be independent. My older sister Courtney has been my confidant and God filter. My younger brother Frankie has been there for me when I didn't know where to turn.

But that doesn't mean that life doesn't get lonely or difficult, because life is messy. There are still days when I feel like I am failing my girls. There are days when I don't know how I'll get it all done. But I can honestly say that I am more content with my life right now than I ever remember being. Not because it is perfect, but because I have learned to be content in whatever my circumstances (Philippians 4:11). I (try to) keep my eyes on Jesus and trust Him. It is a daily choice I make.

There are many things I have learned about myself on this journey, and many I continue to learn. Being a single Mom in a world where it feels like everyone else is married has not always been easy. I have missed out on many things due to lack of money or a baby-sitter for my girls. I isolated myself from others for a while, and thought I had to do it all on my own.

You might be wondering how I got from where I was (isolating myself) to where I am now (content). I am still a single Mom so my situation didn't change...but my perspective did. For example, missing all of those events meant that I got to spend more time with my girls having family game night or movie night. One of the biggest lessons I have learned is that life is about perspective.

Sometimes life feels like a roller coaster...ups, downs, twists, turns. Just when you think you've gotten past a twist, another one may be just around the corner. I have had many of these twists and turns lately, both good and bad, and some can be stressful and scary. For me, as long as I know God is the driver of my roller coaster, I can rest easier in His promises. Does that mean I do not get stressed out, lonely, or scared? Of course not! It means I have comfort for the journey. I have hope when I am stressed or scared. It means I will have peace to be able to sleep at night, and joy in the morning with each new day.

Blessings to you wherever you are in your journey.

You Are Not Alone

Truth #1

Chapter One

"The Lord himself goes before you and will be with you;
he will never leave you nor forsake you.
Do not be afraid; do not be discouraged."
Deuteronomy 31:8

It's two in the morning and your son is throwing up or your daughter can't sleep because of a monster in the closet. Or maybe you have a teenage daughter who wants to start dating, or a son just starting puberty. Who do you turn to when you are the one everyone else is turning to?

This is Truth #1...You are NOT alone! It feels like you are alone. It feels like nobody else in the world is going through what you are. It is easy to become isolated for many reasons. You're single and all of your friends are married. You have children and your other friends do not. Maybe you do not know where you fit.

Let me reassure you that you always have a place with God. He will never leave you or forsake you. He will always be with you. Isaiah 41:10 tells us:

> *So do not fear, for I am with you;*
> *do not be dismayed, for I am your God.*
> *I will strengthen you and help you;*
> *I will uphold you with my righteous right hand.*

I am not sure where you are in your walk with the Lord. Maybe you are just starting your walk with God, or you've been on it for as long as you can remember, or maybe you're somewhere in between. Maybe you picked up this book because you're a single Mom, but now you realize that I am writing about God and you want to put it down...PLEASE DON'T!! Please keep reading! I know this book is for you because GOD is for YOU! It does not matter to God where we are in our walk. He loves us right where we are!

For me, when I became a single Mom, I believed in God, but did not have a relationship with Him. I knew God was there in Heaven, but He was not part of my everyday life. Growing up, there was not a lot of mention of God, except on Christmas and Easter. We never missed a midnight mass. We would also say grace before a meal, but I think it was more of a habit than anything else.

So when I first starting hearing about God's love and promises, and how He wanted to have a relationship with me, I was not sure how to process it all. The fact that people would tell me that God is always with me was foreign to me. It wasn't until an incident that happened involving my youngest daughter showed me the truth. I'm a "neon-sign" kind of girl, so God knew He needed to show me, and He did, in a very big and powerful way.

My youngest daughter has an anxiety disorder, among other special needs. When she was younger, and even still today, she would climb in my bed in the middle of the night to be close to me. One such night when she was about four, she crept into my bed. I was sound asleep when I felt a nudge on my elbow. The poke was hard enough to wake me, but noticing the still of the night, I went right back to sleep. I was awakened again by another nudge to my elbow. Again I woke up, but this time it felt different, so I opened my eyes and that's when I saw it: My elbow. It was covering my little girl's face, almost smothering her. I honestly can't even imagine what would have happened if I had not been woken up.

Did you notice I said 'woken up?' Not that I woke up, because I definitely did not wake up of my own accord. Something or SOMEONE nudged me awake that night. I know, without a single doubt, that God showed up in the middle of the night in my small, two-bedroom duplex, in order to protect my little girl. He showed up. I was not alone. Not then...and not now. And neither are you. *God shows up.*

You only have to look around to see the evidence of Him. Your children are miracles from God. Psalm 139:13 tells us that He "created" them and "knit" them together in their Mother's womb. If that's not a miracle, I don't know what is. But you can look further than your own children, to the fragrant flowers that grow in luscious green grass. Or the sunrise and sunsets that He paints for us each and every day. *God shows up.* He gives us so many signs that we are not alone. One of my favorites is a sign He promised long ago.

I always get excited when I'm reading my Bible and I see the words "God said" or "Jesus said," because I know whatever comes next is HUGE. Not that the rest of the Bible is not, but this is a reminder to me to pay attention because my Savior wants me to know something. It's kind of like when you have an inbox full of emails to go through that are all important,

18

but you see that one from your boss and know it is the one you will answer first.

In Genesis 9:12-13, God makes a promise to Noah...and to all of us. Even though this promise was made many moons ago, the sign is still seen in the sky today.

*And **God said**, "This is the sign of the covenant I am making between me and you and every living creature with you, a covenant for all generations to come: I have set my rainbow in the clouds, and it will be the sign of the covenant between me and the earth. (emphasis added)*

God shows up. When I see the rainbow and all of it's magnificent color in the sky, I am reminded that God is there. He is there and He keeps His promises. It was not an accident that a promise and a sign that He made so long ago would still be around today, for you and me to experience.

I want to make sure I also point out one more miracle, that if not for this particular miracle, you would not be reading this right now. That miracle is YOU. God created you. He loves you. The Bible tells us "And even the very hairs of your head are all numbered." (Matthew 10:30). He knows every single strand of hair on your head...even the ones that are no longer on your head because either stress or a hairbrush has separated them from you.

God shows up. We just have to look for Him. We have to have our eyes and ears open, but more than that, our hearts have to be open. In the midst of being a single Mom, this can be really difficult to do. We've been hurt. We feel alone. I am right there with you. I struggle EVERY. SINGLE. DAY.

Life is hard. Being a mom is hard. Being a single mom is beyond hard. If we had to do this alone, it would be unbearable. I know because I used to think and feel like I was alone. Sometimes I still feel that way. Like when a bunch of people from work are doing date night, but I'm the odd one out because I don't have a date or a babysitter. Or when some other single Mom friends are taking their kiddos to some fun family activity but my girls are with their dad and I don't get to share it with them.

It is so easy to become discouraged if we look around at our circumstances. Mine will be different than yours, and yours will be different from the other single Moms you know. But can I share something really special with you? If we fix our eyes on Jesus, we can stand firm in His love and trust that He will show up....ALWAYS. A great reminder for me, and one I share with my friends so often they probably have it memorized, is found in the book of Joshua.

Have I not commanded you? Be strong and courageous.
Do not be frightened, and do not be dismayed, for the
*Lord your God is with you **wherever you go.***
(Joshua 1:9) (emphasis added)

Can we just take a moment right now and let those last three words soak in. I mean really let it seep into the deepest depths of your heart. Close your eyes and try to grasp the magnitude of this. Can you?

Can I be super honest and transparent with you? Even though I believe this with 100% of my being, there are days that I can't grasp this truth. Those "Mama Fail" days like the one I had today when both of my girls are sick, crabby, and whiny, and this Mama was at the end of her rope. Yep...He is even with me on those days. The difference is that in those moments, I am not with Him. Can you understand the difference?

I did not understand this until a few years ago. I accepted Christ, was baptized, but still felt like something was missing. I thought I wasn't doing something right or I was missing a huge piece of the puzzle. After years of feeling restless and like I just didn't understand this whole being a Christian thing, God led me to a church that opened my eyes and showed me what was missing.

I thought that God would do all the work once I accepted Jesus as my Savior. I incorrectly assumed I didn't need to do anything more. Oh how wrong I was! I am so thankful that God opened my eyes and showed me that while He is always with me, I must be spending time with Him to be able to experience Him. James 4:8a tells us to "Come near to God and he will come near to you."

Do you ever hear a song and it takes you back to when you were a kid or to a great memory? There is a song I hear often, both on the radio and on my iPad at home, that has that effect on me, only in a slightly different way. It definitely is a reminder for me, but it is a reminder that I am not alone. It makes sense that the name of the song is, you guessed it, "I Am Not Alone" by Kari Jobe. If you have never heard this song before, I recommend you stop reading right here and go listen to it. You will be so glad you did.

It is a wonderful reminder that we are definitely NOT alone. Whether it is deep waters, deep sorrows, dark nights, or storms, God is ALWAYS with us. He goes before us and he NEVER leaves us.

So on those days when I'm feeling like I can't wash another dish, fold another piece of laundry, or help with another math problem, I can draw near to God and feel His presence with me. Reminding me that "wherever I go" I am not alone. It almost sounds like it's too good to be true, right? I promise you it's not. I have learned that believing it and applying it to my life are two totally different things.

You are not alone

Truth #1

Go-to verses

Deuteronomy 31:8: "The Lord himself goes before you and will be with you; he will never leave you nor forsake you. Do not be afraid; do not be discouraged."

Joshua 1:9: "Have I not commanded you? Be strong and courageous. Do not be frightened, and do not be dismayed, for the Lord your God is with you wherever you go."

Isaiah 41:10: "So do not fear, for I am with you; do not be dismayed, for I am your God. I will strengthen you and help you; I will uphold you with my righteous right hand"

How to live it out

Applying Truth #1

Chapter Two

We want to experience God and to know that He is with us. How do we do that? I wish I could tell you that I always get it right, but I would be lying. I fail all the time...just ask my girls. They will happily tell you about the time I overreacted because I thought they were bickering yet again, when in reality they were happily playing and laughing together. Or there were those times when my younger daughter who has some special needs was having a sensory meltdown, and instead of remaining calm, this Mama had to take a timeout for myself.

So how can you live out knowing that you are not alone? How can you apply it in your life? The easy answer is to spend time in God's Word. Spend time reading your Bible and praying. The not-so-easy answer is that you have to do what works for you.

In my many years of attempting to get it right, I have discovered five tips to knowing, believing and applying Truth #1 in our lives. These tips seem to be pretty universal to all of us, and how you incorporate these will look different, but the principles are the same. Below are these five tips to applying Truth #1: You Are Not Alone, to your life.

Tip #1 ~ Schedule your quiet time

Life is crazy. It does not matter what age your children are, if you are a single mom, you are acting as two people and your life is crazy. If it's not, feel free to come take some of my crazy! I have found that most people use some type of system or calendar to keep track of things. Take my sister - she is a list-girl. She has lists for her lists. If it is not on one of her lists, it doesn't get done or bought, depending on the list. This works for her. It drives me a little crazy (love you sis!!), but it works for her.

Me, I am more of an electronic calendar kind of girl. I have the calendar on my phone and computer. The same principle applies to my calendar that applies to my sister's lists if it's not on the calendar, it doesn't get done. Maybe you fit into one of these, or maybe you're something different and way more organized than us. The point is, we all have some system to keep track of everything going on. If you do not have a system, I recommend getting one.

So the best way to start implementing quiet time with God is to schedule it like it was any other important meeting or appointment. Maybe you are a morning person, so you start to set your alarm and wake up ten or fifteen minutes before the kiddos and start your day with God. Or if you're like me and a total zombie in the morning, then the evening after the kids are in bed might work better for you.

If you are sitting there thinking there is no way you have any extra time, here is my question to you: can you afford not to schedule time with God? Remember the verse from Truth #1 in James 4:8a: "draw near to God and He will draw near to you." If you want to feel God's presence, you have to spend time with Him.

Tip #2 ~ Read one verse/book at a time

So you have scheduled your quiet time and set your alarm. It is 5am and you sit down in your darkened living room and pull your very large and heavy Bible onto your lap. Now what? When I was first starting out people would tell me to spend time with God, have quiet time with God daily. Okay, that is great and all, but the Bible is a HUGE book and can be overwhelming. So where do you start?

Great question. I have found the best thing to do is to find a verse that you know well and study the book and chapters of the Bible where it is, or to just pick a book of the Bible and start reading it, one chapter at a time. When my twelve-year old daughter came to me with questions, I gave her the same ideas. It has worked well for her, and I think it will for you too.

Tip #3 ~ Turn off the tv, or social media, etc.

Hi my name is Johanna and I am addicted to my tv. I don't even have cable, but I have some local channels and this channel called GRIT plays all kinds of my favorite reruns. For the past month, I have been on a self-imposed tv time-out. I am not saying that you have to sell your tv on eBay or anything, but for me God kept placing Hebrews 12:1 everywhere around me until I got the hint. It says:

Therefore, since we are surrounded by such a great cloud of witnesses, let us throw off everything that hinders and the sin that so easily entangles. And let us run with perseverance the race marked out for us.

For me, the time I spent watching tv was taking the place of the time I spent with God. By turning off my tv I have had so much more time, not just with God but with other things as well. Like writing this book. A lot of this is getting done because I am not occupied with the tv.

Maybe for you it is the tv or maybe you spend two hours a night on social media or a hobby that you have. The point is not that these things are bad, but if you think you do not have time for God, take a look at your daily agenda and really be honest about your time. Can you spare ten minutes a day for your relationship with God?

Tip #4 ~ Find your space

While it is important to schedule time with God and to limit distractions, having a special place where you spend your quiet time with God is important as well. Our "special place" will look different for all of us. For me, I used to do my quiet time sitting on my bed after I tucked my girls in each night. This worked for a while, but then for some reason it wore out its purpose. Now, I sit on the floor in my living room and spend time with God there.

It could be in a small conference room or break room at work. It could be your bedroom or your kitchen table. It could be any place where you are not distracted and can spend time with God. You have to determine the best place for you. God doesn't care where you have your quiet time...He just cares that you do.

Tip #5 ~ Be flexible

Both of my girls are sick right now. This throws a wrench in my plans because they need more of me than they normally do. So last night I did not have my normal quiet time, and that is okay. I can't make a habit of missing my time with God, because I can definitely tell a difference, but when things come up and I am needed, I have to be flexible.

When we are the only ones here to take care of our children and attend to their needs, we have to allow ourselves grace (sneak peek at an upcoming truth!). In the same regard, we can't let our quiet time slide. To make up for not being able to do my quiet time last night, I did a short devotion in my car this morning when we got to the doctor's office. This helped to start my day off right.

You will find that these are not an exact science, and as I've said, what works for one may not work for another. It's not a cookie-cutter process that can be applied universally. It may take some trial and error to find what works best for you, and what works best in this season may change for next season. As long as you are open to God and are spending time regularly soaking in His Word, you're on the right track to experiencing Him and feeling like you are not alone.

Life Application Check-Up
Truth #1: You are not alone

Truth check-ups are questions to get you thinking about how you are applying these truths to your life. Be honest with yourself and as always, there is NO JUDGEMENT. I promise.

1. Intimate relationships become intimate when we invest our time. It can be very difficult because it means we have to be intentional. Based on the times you have connected with God this week, would you say that you know for sure "He is with you?"

2. What are some ways you can know for sure?

3. Is there a specific time of day you connect with God?

4. What would it look like for you to be more intentional this week?

5. What was your biggest takeaway from this chapter?

God Loves Your Child(ren)

Truth #2

Chapter Three

Then he put a little child among them. Taking the child in his arms, he said to them, "Anyone who welcomes a little child like this on my behalf welcomes me, and anyone who welcomes me welcomes not only me but also my Father who sent me."

Mark 9:36-37

When I first looked into the beautiful, wide blue eyes of my daughter Andrea when she was born, I knew nobody on earth could love her like I did. My heart was overflowing with more love than I ever thought I could feel. It was one of the best moments of my life.

Maybe you can relate? As Mamas, we love our children more than life itself. We are their Moms and however God blessed us with them, whether we carried them or adopted them, they are a part of us. Let me share some big truth with you today: God loves them even MORE than we do. Say WHAT?!?!

I know….this is probably the most difficult truth for me to believe and live out. And I have to remind myself of this truth EVERY. SINGLE. DAY. No joke. It is a daily thing I have to surrender to God.

I remember very clearly the very first time I surrendered my girls to Him. I was sitting outside the building that would later become my younger daughter's preschool and kindergarten. As I mentioned before, she has some special needs and I had requested the school evaluate her for services. I was a researching machine...no lie. I literally did anything and everything I could think of to make sure she would get the help she desperately needed. But up until that moment, I had forgotten the most important thing...God.

I didn't completely forget about Him, because He is a huge part of our lives, but in this instance, I was taking all of the pressure and work on myself. So as I sat there in the car with the sun beating down on me and the air-conditioner blowing in my face, I prayed. I knew that I wanted to pray before I went in, so that I could invite God into the meeting and to give us all wisdom to know what was best for my little girl.

As I sat there and closed my eyes, they filled with tears as I realized that I had done everything I could possibly do to control the situation, but God was in control. He already had everything worked out for my daughter. So as I sat there, I cried out to God with this prayer:

"Dear Lord ~ I can't do this by myself anymore. I need you. I need Your help and Your guidance. Please be with me in this meeting today. Lord ~ I surrender Alexa to You. I put her in Your hands, and I trust whatever the outcome of this meeting is, because I know You already have it worked out and have a plan for her. Thank You for loving us. I love You Jesus, Amen."

And praise God the meeting went perfectly...exactly how I wanted it to go, with the services I knew my daughter needed. That meeting four years ago started a long journey that we are all still on...and we are not in it alone. God is always with us, loving us, and loving our children.

But how do we KNOW that God loves our children? That's a great question, and an important one. When it has anything to do with my kiddos, I need some kind of proof. The meeting I just mentioned was kind of the start for me, but I wanted to know more. When I want to know more about God, I go right to the source...God and His Word. So what does the Bible say about children?

Matthew 19:14 tells us "Jesus said, "Let the little children come to me, and do not hinder them, for the kingdom of heaven belongs to such as these."" This verse in itself tells us a lot, because it tells us that Jesus allowed the children to come to Him. For me though, when I add the verse right before this one, it gives it even more meaning.

Then the little children were brought to Jesus for Him to place His hands on them and pray for them; and the disciples rebuked those who brought them.
Matthew 19:13.

Have you ever been to a wedding reception, party, work picnic, or any type of event where the invitation specifically suggests that it is for adults only? Well, that makes things extra difficult for us as single Moms because we may have our children most, if not all of the time. So it can put us in a tough spot because we might want to go, but may not be able to. I do understand it is their event and their right to have it adults only. But that doesn't always make it easy.

In Matthew 19:13, the apostles did the exact same thing. They tried to make it adults only to talk to Jesus. Jesus set them straight and at the same time, showed us that He values the little children and He wants us to come to Him like they do.

Recently Hurricane Matthew has been wreaking havoc on the coast of Florida where a friend of mine, Bethany, lives. Her family had to board up and leave their home to go stay in a shelter. I can't imagine how scary this was for her two young sons. I want to share a story she posted about one of her sons and his faith in God. Let this be a reminder that God DOES love and value our children, and WANTS them to come to Him.

"God, give me faith like a child.

After cleaning-up dog poop for over 2 hours this morning in the dark with the boys, I decided it was time to go to McDonalds for lunch. We ran into many of our neighbors there - all about as tired as we were from peanut butter sandwiches. We swapped hurricane stories and all were wondering when our area of Palm Bay would get electric again. It seemed as if everyone was on except for us!

Then my 6 year-old spoke up - 'Mom, didn't you ask Jesus to turn on our electricity?'

Honestly, my initial thought was - I just asked Him to move the hurricane away and He definitely did that, I think electricity isn't quite as important.

But he saw my hesitation and sighed. 'Really mom? I have to do everything!' Then he prayed:

'Jesus, thank you for the food. Turn on our electric when we get back home, ok? Ok! Thank You! Amen!'

I asked Caden, 'Why did you ask Jesus to turn on our electric AFTER we got home? Why not right now?'

He answered immediately - 'Cause I want to turn the light on!'

We did our playland thing and my jaw dropped as I saw a FPL (Florida Power and Light) truck drive by. Seriously - what's the chance??

When our van pulled in the driveway, I barely parked before Caden was bolting out of the door. 'Come on mom - hurry up!' Silently I was making deals with God - please give my son this moment!

The front door unlocked.

Caden bolted in and tinkered with every switch in the house on his level.

Nada.

Awesome. So then we talked about how sometimes God works in His timing, not ours. Caden's head hung low.

As we were loading the van to head back to our evening a/c - Caden spotted the porch light - ON!

Before I even had a second to react I heard - 'Mom, He did it! He did it! Look mom! He did it!'

Every single light and fan in our house works. With every click of a switch, Caden's laughter could be heard screeching through our house. I could not quit laughing. It was just one of those awesome moments as a mom I will never forget.

Don't think even the small things are overlooked by God. He sees. He knows. He provides and He reminds us to come to him with the faith like a child, expecting our Abba Daddy to provide.

Back to cleaning (Caden can't pray himself out of that one!)."

Is this powerful truth awesome or what?!? Jesus wanted the children to come to Him, like He wanted Bethany's to come to Him, like He wants OURS to come to Him. I hope that gives you as much reassurance and hope as it gives me. But wait...there's more!! (sorry...I've always wanted to be able to say that!!).

The very next verse in Matthew is more proof that Jesus loves our children. Do you know how I know this? I know this because verse 15 says "And after He had placed His hands on them, He went on from there." AFTER He had placed His hands on them He left. He didn't just let the children come to Him and say hi. He had a purpose for letting them come. He laid His hands on them and blessed them! That is HUGE for me as a Mom because this applies to our children today! God blesses every single one of them!!!

Are you ready for some more truth about how God feels about our children? Let's read a few more verses in Matthew. This time we will be in Matthew 18:1-5:

> *At that time the disciples came to Jesus, saying,*
> *"Who is the greatest in the kingdom of heaven?"*
> *And calling to him a child, he put him in the midst*
> *of them and said, "Truly, I say to you, unless you*
> *turn and become like children, you will never enter*
> *the kingdom of heaven. Therefore, whoever takes*
> *the lowly position of this child is the greatest in the*

*kingdom of heaven. And whoever welcomes one
such child in my name welcomes me.*

Okay let's stop right there and read that again. Let it penetrate your heart and stay there. In His own Words, Jesus proclaims that children are the "greatest in the kingdom of heaven." Say WHAT?!? He does not leave any doubt about this.

As a Mama, this soothes my soul. This right here calms my heart. What about you? Precious friends, I am praying that this right here is something that you can take with you as you wait in the car line, clean up the spill yet again, walk the floor with a crying baby, worry about academics and friends, or whatever life situation you are in right this very moment. Jesus loves our children.

God loves your child(ren)

Truth #2

Go-to verses

Matthew 19:13: "Then the little children were brought to Jesus for Him to place His hands on them and pray for them; and the disciples rebuked those who brought them."

Matthew 18:1-5: "At that time the disciples came to Jesus, saying, "Who is the greatest in the kingdom of heaven?" And calling to him a child, he put him in the midst of them and said, "Truly, I say to you, unless you turn and become like children, you will never enter the kingdom of heaven. Therefore, whoever takes the lowly position of this child is the greatest in the kingdom of heaven. And whoever welcomes one such child in my name welcomes me."

How to live it out

Applying Truth #2

Chapter Four

Knowing something and *believing in* something aren't exactly the same concept, and it will not be the same for all of us. Maybe your children are adult children living on their own, or you're still changing diapers, wondering if it ever ends. Whatever your current walk in life, here are five tips to help you live out Truth #2: God Loves Your Children.

Tip #1 ~ Surrender

I absolutely think the first step is surrender. Not just daily surrender to God, but the daily surrender of **our children** to God. I know this may seem scary, even impossible. We are their Mamas and we know what is best. But God.

God knows even better than our best. Trust me, I have to remind myself of this every single day. My thought process is "I'm their Mom and nobody knows them and loves them like I do." So Mamas...the struggle is real!! I'm right there with you.

So how do we live out Truth #2: God Loves Our Children? What does it look like to surrender them to Jesus daily? Let go. Let go of control. We can't control everything that happens to our children or the choices they make...no matter how old or what stage of life they are in. Have you ever tried to control a 2-year old who sees the cookie jar has cookies in it??? Not happening!! I know my Mom would tell you that trying to tell a headstrong adult child something is like talking to a wall. I'm sure she was talking about my sister though...

We feel like we always have to be "on" and ready to help our children fix all of their problems, because it is just the role of being a parent. We are all they have. But we *aren't* all they have, and we are not alone. Remember Truth #1? It applies to both us and our children.

Tip #2 ~ Training

Recently a friend that I work with was training for a half-marathon. I'll never understand the desire to run thirteen miles for fun. I'm tired just thinking about it. But she enjoys it and that's awesome. She had been training for months, but things kept happening.

Setbacks. The enemy attacking. Sprained ankle. Crutches. Things that would definitely hinder her training. She could have easily given up when things got tough, but she didn't. She persevered and did what the doctor ordered, and was able to run and complete her race.

There is a lesson in her story that applies to training our children and giving them life tools. I guarantee you there will be setbacks, and they may even include crutches. But like my friend, if we give up, we will not be able to complete what God has laid before us- to equip our children to love Jesus and others, regardless of what life throws at them.

Train up a child in the way he should go; even when
he is old he will not depart from it.
Proverbs 22:6

Tip #3 ~ Prayer

Prayer is our most powerful tool. Coming before God and sharing our prayers is what He wants from us. No prayer is too big or too small for God. We have to trust Him and pray for our children. Pray for ourselves. Take the next right step. Make the next RIGHT choice.

These will not be the same steps for all of us. For me, my girls are thirteen and nine, so allowing Andrea (my thirteen year old) the freedom to choose her own friends and organize her own time after school is a step I need to take...a step without trying to control any of it. I have equipped her, and I continue to equip her, with tools to grow in her own relationship with Jesus and in life. It is up to her to use them.

Now Alexa, my nine year old, does not yet have these freedoms and choices to make. Eventually she will, but in our current season, I am more involved. Whether our children are at home with us, at college, married, or out living on their own, they need our prayers. They have to make decisions every day, and they NEED us to be praying for them.

Tip #4 ~ Love them like Jesus does

Jesus' love is perfect. The only perfect love in the entire world. We are so blessed to experience His love and we need to show this same love to our children. I know you might be thinking there is no way we can love perfectly, because only Jesus was perfect, and you're right. But we can certainly try our hardest. If anyone deserves for us to give it our all, our children do.

Jesus was patient. Heck, He wanted His friends to pray with Him and they kept falling asleep!! (Matthew 26:40). Even then He loved them and didn't leave them. And He doesn't leave us. We all fall short and fail every day (Romans 3:23), yet He loves us. We need to be patient with our children, and show them that same love.

Tip #5 ~ Don't get in God's way

If you looked up 'helicopter parent' in the dictionary, you would probably see a picture of me. Seriously, picture the Mom constantly chasing after the little girl, making sure she doesn't fall, make a mess, or good grief...cry!! Yep, that was me. Back then I was a worrier...back then before Jesus.

Today I can say that I try REALLY hard not to be that Mom anymore. There are times that it still creeps up, but I'm getting better at giving it to God. This is because I have realized that I keep getting in God's way.

I know, right?!? But I'm serious. God has his own plan for my daughters' lives, and I have to stay out of His way. If I am trying to 'handle' things (come on...nobody likes that bad c word...you know, control!). If I'm trying to 'handle' things, it means God is not able to do the work in them He is trying to do.

I don't know about y'all, but I do NOT want to get in His way. I want Him to do His will in their lives. I want them to experience Him, and if I keep getting in the way, they might not have that intimate experience, and that is just not acceptable.

Life Application Check-Up

Truth #2: God loves your child(ren)

Truth check-ups are questions to get you thinking about how you are applying these truths to your life. Be as honest as you can and as always, there is NO JUDGEMENT. I promise.

1. Is there any area in your child(ren)'s lives you need to surrender to God?

2. What is one way you can show grace to your child(ren) this week?

3. What was your biggest takeaway from this chapter?

Community Is Important

Truth #3

Chapter Five

How good and pleasant it is

when God's people live together in unity!

Psalm 133:1

It was all over social media. Friends were out enjoying the beautiful fall weather. Football games. Movies. And of course my favorite...bonfires. Seeing my friends experience life, while I sat at home with my girls made me feel sad. Don't get me wrong...there is NO place I would rather be than spending time with my girls. But it is still hard to see everyone else having a great time living it up while I am at home, feeling isolated. Being a single Mom can make us feel isolated because maybe we don't feel like we relate, or we don't want people to feel uncomfortable or upset because we bring our children with us. Sometimes our isolation is our choice, and other times it is beyond our control.

When Alexa was younger, her special needs were such that I could not take her to a lot of different places. This was back before her multiple diagnosis'. I did not know what to do or how to help her stop having meltdowns when we would be out. So honestly, my isolation was partly due to my daughter's needs, but partly because I did not want to deal with all of it. So I stayed home and would watch tv or scroll on social media once they were fast asleep.

Maybe you face these same challenges, or maybe you are feeling isolated because you don't know where you fit. Or you're embarrassed or feeling guilty because you are a single Mom. I am not sure what is driving your isolation, but I so wish I could sit across from you and speak so much truth to you that your heart is overflowing with it.

Since that is not an option, I'm going to lay some truth out for you right now. It does not matter what your life circumstances are, God does not want us to do life alone. How do I know? I know because Matthew tells us in Chapter 18:

"For where two or three gather in my
name, there am I with them."
Matthew 18:20

God is with us when we are together with other people!!
He is in it with us!

I realize this may seem scary to you, or even impossible...but NOTHING is impossible with God (Matthew 19:26)! Can I get an AMEN?! We will talk in the next chapter about how to get connected, but first I would like to share part of my story with you.

Remember when I said I was isolated and did not get out much? That did not stop God from connecting me to other "Jesus-lovin'" girls. One of those nights I was alone at home while my girls slept and I was scrolling through social media. I came across this picture advertising an online Bible study. At the time, I was not able to go to a Bible study at church, so this intrigued me. It gave me hope.

That was over three years and many, many Bible studies ago. I even became a volunteer for the online Bible studies and I made some amazing friends. I know God had me right where He wanted me - on my couch, scrolling through social media just so I could see that picture. He has you right where He wants you too.

Maybe you are already connected, and that is awesome!! I don't want you to think this truth skips or doesn't apply to you, because it does. God does have you right where He wants you and right now that means reading this book. Maybe in the next chapter you will find some new ways to connect, so please keep reading. Maybe something you read will help you help another single Mom God places in your path.

Not only are we supposed to be in community, but we should be encouraging one another.

"And let us consider how we may spur one another on toward love and good deeds, not giving up meeting together, as some are in the habit of doing, but encouraging one another"
Hebrews 10:24-25a

We should be meeting together, encouraging one another, and spurring each other on towards love. This verse encompasses what it means to do life in community and to get connected.

I know this may not be easy for some of you. It was not easy for me at first either, and I still struggle sometimes with isolating myself. I think it is healthy to have some alone time, and I'm not suggesting you spend every second in community. But having community around you and being connected with other Jesus-lovin' girls is important.

Being a single Mom often means being fiercely protective of our children. We do not want to expose them to people we are not sure that we can count on. At the same time, having them with us is almost like a safety net, at least for me. When I first joined the Single Parent Family Ministry at a new (very large) church, I always felt more comfortable if my girls were with me. I could focus on them and not interact too much with the other parents.

Looking back, I can admit that I hid behind them because it was safer. It was easier. It was comfortable. I was basically isolating myself in community. Talk about an oxymoron! I was allowing fear to dictate my interactions in community. Mamas...one of the reasons I am writing this book is to reveal my experience and to equip you to make great choices!

The Single Parent Family Ministry I just wrote about? I served as part of the planning team for it for a while. Only God could take me from where I was to where I am now. He can take you to amazing places too...but first you have to take a step. Are you ready? Check out the tips to getting connected in the next chapter. You will be glad you did!!

Community is important

Truth #3

Go-to verses

Matthew 19:26: "Jesus looked at them and said, "With man this is impossible, but with God all things are possible.""

Matthew 18:20: "For where two or three gather in my name, there am I with them."

Hebrews 10:24-25a: "And let us consider how we may spur one another on toward love and good deeds, not giving up meeting together, as some are in the habit of doing, but encouraging one another."

How to live it out

Applying Truth #3

Chapter Six

Have you ever walked into a room and you just knew that you didn't belong? This was me about four years ago. My girls and I started attending this giant church...well, it felt giant at the time. There were so many people that it was almost overwhelming. But I truly felt God was calling me there, so we continued to go.

I started off going to the singles class for my age group, but it was not long before I realized the people in the class and I had totally different lifestyles. They did all of these amazing things, like ice cream after class and weekend retreats, but I had my girls and was not able to really go to anything.

This was when I first found out about the Single Parent Family Ministry I was talking about in the last chapter. What a true blessing this has been. I know it can be scary, but getting connected is vital for us if we want to become the best Moms we can be for our kiddos...and they definitely deserve our best!

So you might be thinking...okay that's great she found that, but my church doesn't have that. Or maybe you don't go to church. There are so many different ways to get connected. Here are five tips to help you live out Truth #3: Community Is Important.

Tip #1 ~ Start Small

Start small. Give yourself a small, attainable goal to reach out to one person. Maybe you have a circle of friends and you still feel alone, or maybe you are like I was and are pretty isolated whether by location or circumstance. So start small.

If you attend a church, send an email to the Women's Director and ask her the ways to get connected. If you do not attend a church, my best friend Google is always good for options. Do an internet search for churches in your area. Start small.

Don't try to jump all in if you are not ready, but you will have to take a step. Even if you are scared. Even if you are uncomfortable. God does some of His best work when we are out of our comfort zones. We have to then rely solely on Him.

You got this Mama!! You CAN do it!! I wish I was sitting across from you, cheering you on, telling you I believe in you and I know you can do it. Trust me...if I could do it, so can you! So what is your small step going to be today?

Tip #2 ~ Ask God

I know, I know...I should have put this as the first tip, because going to God is always the first thing you should do. As you can see, I often fail in this area, but I'm a work in progress and God is working on me!

So...ask God. Pray and ask God to show you an opportunity to connect. Here is something I have found to be so important when we ask God for something: We have to be ready to listen!! Again, this is another area where I struggle. Hmm...maybe I should go back and start this one over. Nope...I believe in keeping it real, and y'all...this is as real as it gets!

When you ask God for something, you may not get an answer right away. Maybe you will feel like He is not listening, but I promise you He is. God is always working, even when we do not see it. Not only is He working, but He has a plan for your life. Jeremiah 29:11 tells us:

"For I know the plans I have for you," declares the LORD, "plans to prosper you and not to harm you, plans to give you hope and a future."

When He does answer, God may show you a link to something on social media. Maybe a friend will invite you to a family-friendly activity. When you ask God to bring you an opportunity, be ready to take that step. And remember Truth #1...when you do take that step, You are NOT alone!!

Tip #3 ~ Online Bible Studies

God does not want us to do life alone. He wants us to do life together. He designed us to do life in community. The enemy wants us separated and isolated so that we doubt ourselves and our worth and turn away from God. But God is so faithful and He will guide you. He already knows where and with whom you are going to connect. Are you willing and ready to take a step?

If you do not think you are ready for a full Bible study or to connect with people in person, then go online. There are online Bible study communities for women that are such a blessing. You build relationships not only with other women, but with God!

Are you intrigued? Do you want to know more? YAY!!! That's great!! I promise you it is very simple to find an online Bible study and to sign up. The information comes directly to your inbox. You can be as involved as you'd like. You tailor it to suit your current season of life.

Does it sound too good to be true? Well guess what?? It's NOT!! I have been a part of online Bible studies for more than three years and I LOVE it!! So I encourage you, if this has sparked an interest for you, to check it out!

Tip #4 ~ Serve

We have three main words that our church focuses on for us. They are love, grow, and serve. I feel like sometimes the last one, serve, is the most difficult to live out. We are too busy...especially as single moms, with so much going on. Maybe we feel that God can't use us, or that people will judge us.

Can I share something with you? God can use ALL of us. We just have to be open to letting Him. Remember, it does not have to be a long-term commitment. Maybe you donate old clothes and shoes to a women's shelter. Maybe you are an amazing baker and you can bless someone with cookies. There is something YOU can do to serve others. You just have to find what works for you.

Tip #5 ~ Start a Bible study

If all else fails and you just are not finding a way to connect, then start your own Bible study for single Moms at your house. This is what I have done. I reached out to some other single Moms and asked them if they were interested in doing a Bible study.

It worked well for us because the kids could all come, so we did not have to worry about a babysitter. We each brought a snack to share, if we could. The best part was that we tailored it to meet our needs, so that we were still able to connect.

Life Application Check-Up

Truth #3: Community is important

Truth check-ups are questions to get you thinking about how you are applying these truths to your life. Be as honest as you can and as always, there is NO JUDGEMENT. I promise.

1. On a scale of one to ten, with ten being the most connected, what would you rate your current level of community?

2. What is one thing you can do this week to get more connected, or to help another single mom get connected?

3. Is something holding you back from being more connected? Pray and ask God to reveal any areas that might be stopping you.

4. What was your biggest takeaway from this chapter?

Grace, Grace, Grace

Truth #4

Chapter Seven

But he said to me, "My grace is sufficient for you, for my power is made perfect in weakness." Therefore I will boast all the more gladly about my weaknesses, so that Christ's power may rest on me.

2 Corinthians 12:9

You finally go into your bedroom and close the door because you know after that debacle you need a Mommy time-out. The kids are bickering again, they haven't cleaned their room like you told them five times, and you finally blew your top. Sound familiar? I know I can speak on this from very personal experience.

There have been so many times when the stress gets to me and I just can't take it. So I go in my room and close the door. I would love to sit here and tell you that I never slam it but I would be lying. You'd think there were three kids living in this house instead of two. But there it is. I'm praying you've been there so I won't feel judgement staring back at me as you're reading this!

Although I DO feel judgement...judgement from myself. Guilt that starts to eat at my stomach as I am sitting in my Mommy time-out. This is prime feeding ground for the enemy because he knows as a single Mom, we take all the blame. There is nobody else in the house. Just us. That is not a very good place to be...not at all.

My girls and I LOVE Christian music blaring on the radio. Okay if I'm being honest, I love to blare it...they like to listen at human levels. So we compromised and turn it up when our favorites come on. One of those favorites is "Grace Wins Every Time" by Matthew West.

I think this started because our church is called Grace Church, so we think this should be like our anthem or something. So we love to belt out "Grace Wins Every Time" when the chorus comes on. Lately I have been listening to the other lyrics. I think they ring so true for us. If you are not familiar with the song, it talks about a war going on between guilt and grace.

I truly believe there is a war going on inside each and every one of us Moms. We may feel guilt because our kid's father is not in the picture, or maybe he is and we feel guilt because we have given our children a broken home. It could be that we feel guilty because we think they would have a better life and more stuff if our home was a two-parent home. Or maybe it is day to day guilt. The house isn't clean enough. We missed their activity. We overreacted. Gosh my list could go on and on.

This is why I love this song so much because it is a reminder that grace does win EVERY TIME. Not just sometimes or once in awhile...but EVERY TIME! So maybe right now you're wondering what I mean by grace. According to my best friend Google, one of the definitions is:

> "(in Christian belief) the free and unmerited favor of God, as manifested in the salvation of sinners and the bestowal of blessings."

God forgives us and shows us grace. Google also gives a synonym for grace - acceptance. God accepts us. If we love Him and follow His will, he accepts us. He meets us right where we are...in our bedroom or the bathroom, in our Mommy time-out. He meets us right there and He gives us grace. Grace to say we are sorry. Grace to keep moving forward. Grace to be forgiven. Grace Wins!

For it is by grace you have been saved, through faith—and this is not from yourselves, it is the gift of God—
Ephesians 2:8

We are not perfect. We all have strengths and weaknesses. My least favorite question to be asked in an interview is "What is your biggest weakness?" Do they really want to know? I don't think so. I think they want to know how we can put a positive spin on it. "My biggest weakness is that I am a perfectionist and I always want to make sure every detail is right, BUT I am working on overcoming this by (insert positive phrase here)."

As a Mom, we WANT desperately to be that perfect Mom. You know the one. She is at every party, every field trip. All of her favors and treats are Pinterest worthy. Her hair is always in perfect place. Her clothes are fashionable. And let's not even talk about her shoes. Oh girl! (by the way...I LOVE this Mom because she adds so much to the parties!)

But here is the thing about that Mom...she is not perfect either. Maybe her strength is fashion-sense and creativity. Me, I'm a t-shirt and jeans kind of girl...ask anyone who knows me.

I don't think I would know fashion-sense if it jumped out and bit me. But I have many other strengths.

When we can accept and acknowledge our weaknesses and give them to God, He tells us:

> *But he said to me, "My grace is sufficient for you, for my power is made perfect in weakness." Therefore I will boast all the more gladly about my weaknesses, so that Christ's power may rest on me.*
> *2 Corinthians 12:9*

God does His best work in the midst of our weaknesses. When we can overcome a situation by giving it to God, He is able to use that for His glory and for our strength. God's grace is sufficient for us. God's grace gives us hope because it tells us we do not have to be perfect.

When I was in middle school, I loved to get good grades. I tried hard and my grades showed it, because they were all A's. Then one day I got my report card (this was WAY before we can just view them daily online like I can my daughters' now) and there was this letter I had never seen before on my report card. It was a B! I couldn't believe I had a B. I was so mad at myself, wondering what I could have done differently or better. I know...big stress for a sixth grader.

However, my Mom was still proud of me because she knew I had tried my best that quarter, and let's keep it real: a B is a good grade. Nothing wrong with a B. For me there was, and I was so upset with myself. I did not give myself much grace in this situation...or other situations like it.

Giving grace to ourselves is difficult most of the time, but it is so important. If God can give us grace, why can't we give it to ourselves? I can't imagine we have higher standards than God Himself. So what would it look like if we gave ourselves grace? If grace really did win in the middle of our mess?

You know that Mama in a self-imposed Mommy time-out? With grace, as she sits in that room all alone, she prays to God and asks for forgiveness. She thanks God for being there with her and for His forgiveness, and for His grace. But she doesn't stop there. You see, we can't just say we are going to do it, we have to live it out and show it to our children. If we don't, who will?

Last year I was taking a Single & Parenting class at church. It was a really good class and a bunch of other single Moms I knew were in the class. One of them, who is now a good friend of mine, shared a story about how she overreacted with her son when he went to cross the street without looking. Been there...done that. I think fear makes our voices harsher and louder than we intend.

Then she shared with us how she handled it with her son. She told us that she knelt down, hugged him, and apologized. I was thinking, okay, I've done this. It was what she told us next that really changed things for me. She said they prayed together and asked God for forgiveness right then and there.

Talk about a light bulb moment for me. I started doing this at home with my girls, and it's gotten to the point where Alexa will now ask me to pray with her to ask for forgiveness. How awesome is that?? If she had not seen me do it first, she would have never known to do it for herself. This is a great example of community we talked about in the last chapter, and having people to fellowship with and share ideas.

So back to the Mom in time-out. She goes in her kids' room and asks them for forgiveness, and then asks them to pray with her. She not only gives herself grace in the moment, but she is teaching her children to not only give grace to themselves, but to others as well.

God wants us to come to Him. He tells us in Hebrews 4:16:

"Let us then approach God's throne of grace with confidence, so that we may receive mercy and find grace to help us in our time of need."

We should approach Him with confidence! He wants to help us in our time of need by giving us grace. By not coming to Him, we are depriving Him of extending His grace.

Think of it this way: would you want your child to not come to you about something when you knew you could make them feel better? Of course not! God feels the same way about us. He wants us to come to Him for grace so He can help us.

Not only does He want us to come to Him for grace, but He wants us to show grace to others. 1 Peter 4:10 gives this direction:

"Each of you should use whatever gift you have received to serve others, as faithful stewards of God's grace in its various forms."

We should serve others with grace. That doesn't just mean our children, but it includes everyone we come in contact with. That means the guy taking forever in the checkout line in front of us while our child is screaming. It also means the cashier who gave us the wrong change and now we have to go to customer service and get it corrected. And yes, it even includes those people who cut us off while we are driving because they chose to ignore the "left lane closed ahead sign."

Grace wins. Not just for me. Not just for you. Not just for our children. Grace wins every time for everyone. So show yourself a little grace today. You deserve it.

Grace, Grace, Grace

Truth #4

Go-to verses

2 Corinthians 12:9: "But he said to me, "My grace is sufficient for you, for my power is made perfect in weakness." Therefore I will boast all the more gladly about my weaknesses, so that Christ's power may rest on me."

Hebrews 4:16: "Let us then approach God's throne of grace with confidence, so that we may receive mercy and find grace to help us in our time of need."

1 Peter 4:10: "Each of you should use whatever gift you have received to serve others, as faithful stewards of God's grace in its various forms."

How to live it out

Applying Truth #4

Chapter Eight

If you're anything like me, you still can't get past having to show grace to that person who cut you off. It's not my fault they chose to ignore the huge sign back there that said "LEFT LANE CLOSED AHEAD." I know they ignored it on purpose because they wanted to get in front of everyone. How dare them!

Hmm...that does not seem very gracious of me does it? Maybe their Mom is in the hospital and they have to get there right away. Maybe they are meeting their husband at the lab because he is having testing. Or maybe they are just acting like a jerk. The point is, I have no idea what is going on in their mind or their life, but I do not get to choose if I show grace.

God shows me grace every day and I don't deserve it. Every.Single.Day. For real! It is not my job to worry about what the person in that car, or that grocery line, or on the other end of that phone is thinking or dealing with. It IS my job to do what God wants me to do, and that is to show others that grace wins.

So how do we do that? How do we live out this truth of showing grace to others and to ourselves? Let's dig into these five tips I have found that help to live out Truth #4: Grace, Grace, Grace.

Tip #1 ~ Slow down and breathe

I know...you see the words slow down and you start to panic because you can't slow down. You have too much to do. Too many things on your list and on your plate. Okay now breathe in. Breathe out.

If we want to be able to extend grace to others and accept it ourselves, we need to slow down enough to process life. If you go go go, you will not have the capacity to extend grace because you will be rung out. I am speaking from experience...very real this past weekend experience. I think this was the busiest weekend we've had all year.

From Andrea's musical at school, to Youth Gatherings at Church, a birthday party, Single Mom Fellowship event, church service...and I haven't even gotten to laundry, cleaning, feeding the little people in my house who need to eat. See what I mean? I'll be honest....this was NOT a good weekend for us.

I overscheduled us and we all paid for it. I did not extend much grace to anyone, and I definitely did not extend it to myself.

I definitely learned a lesson...okay I learned it AGAIN, that I need to slow down. If I am going to extend grace to myself and those around me, I need to be able to step back and take a breath. If I am going full speed ahead all the time, I will most certainly miss opportunities to show grace. I don't want that for my children and I don't want that for myself. So I must slow down.

Tip #2 ~ Have an accountability partner

Accountability. This is such an important thing but I think it is not utilized nearly enough. Right now, an amazing friend of mine is mentoring me through the Titus 2 mentoring program. For this season of my life, she is my accountability partner. We meet once a month to discuss the program and that month's book. It works for me in this season.

I have also had accountability partners when I wanted to start getting healthier and drink more water. We would text each other throughout the day, or sometimes once a day, to check our progress. It was simple and it worked for us.

Having an accountability partner does not have to be something that takes up a lot of your time. The great thing is you can make it whatever you want it to be. You could have a playdate with your kids and talk then. It could be as simple as someone sending you a text that reads "Have you given yourself Grace today?" Just a daily or weekly reminder to accept and extend grace.

Tip #3 ~ Give yourself reminders

It's five o'clock in the evening and you are cooking dinner. The kids are bickering again in the other room and you hear a loud crash. You're already stressed and you go in there and see a huge mess and you yell at them to clean it up RIGHT. THIS. INSTANT. You return to the kitchen feeling defeated, like you failed yet again. Right at that moment your phone buzzes an alert and it only displays one word: "GRACE."

I love my calendar. My daughters know that if it is not on my calendar, it's not going to happen. I try to make sure there is lots of white space (usually) so that I have free time to be spontaneous with my girls when I can, but my calendar is what keeps me on track with things for work, home, school, and doctors. But it can be used for other things as well.

Like in my illustration above, you can remind yourself once a day, once an hour, once a week...whatever you need that works for you. Just seeing the word grace come across your phone is a good reminder for yourself. You can even add a Bible verse notation with it, as an additional reminder of God's grace.

Tip #4 ~ Go to God's word

Speaking of Bible verses....go to God's Word. Not only will you find numerous verses about grace, but you will also find stories of grace, forgiveness, mercy...and the list goes on. This is God's love letter to us. The life story of His Son to be an example of how we should live.

Reading God's Word will not only help you to understand His grace, it will also help you to grow closer to Him, which will help you to show grace more often. I think you get the picture. Spending time reading God's Word has a domino effect on our lives. I notice a difference in myself when I haven't spent time with God, and I also notice it in my 13-year-old daughter, Andrea.

God's Word is a powerful tool He has given us to help us in every season, every valley, every celebration. Every. Single. Moment. Why wouldn't we turn to Him and His Word?

Tip #5 ~ Take a Mommy Time-Out

So I know I have written about a Mommy Time-Out and maybe it seemed like a negative thing. I think in the moment it felt like a negative thing because I had to take it AFTER I freaked out. The thing with a Mommy Time-Out is that it gives us a break, whether it is after an argument with our kids or before.

Maybe we know we have to have an important conversation with our children, like about sex or drugs or boys, or anything else. Taking a Mommy Time-Out before this will better prepare us to have this talk. We can show grace to them in our conversation and with our words.

Or....maybe you just overreacted with your kids and you just need five minutes to yourself. That's okay too. Acknowledging you need that five minutes is huge. Let's face it...some of you reading this can't even get five minutes alone in the bathroom? Can I get an amen?!?

We need to take the time alone when we can or when we desperately need it because it is important. We have to take care of ourselves so that we can take care of everyone else. If this means you close your door, or barricade it if you have to, so that you can show grace to yourself and your children, then you should do it.

Life Application Check-Up

Truth #4: Grace, Grace, Grace

Truth check-ups are questions to get you thinking about how you are applying these truths to your life. Be as honest as you can and as always, there is NO JUDGEMENT. I promise.

1. In what ways this week have you shown yourself grace?

2. Which one of the five tips could you start today, to show yourself grace?

3. Is there an area of your life where you do not think you deserve grace?

4. What was your biggest takeaway from this chapter?

The Importance of Self and Soul-Care

Truth #5

Chapter Nine

"Come to me, all you who are weary and burdened,
and I will give you rest."
Matthew 11:28

As single Moms, we take care of everyone. We take the kids to games, practices, school choir concerts. We do the laundry, wash the dishes, clean the house. I could go on and on...and on and on. This does not even touch the list of emotional things we have to deal with.

Being the mom of a teenager, I am in the trenches with puberty and emotions and everything that goes along with that. It can be very stressful, and being the only parent in the house can add to that stress. There isn't someone here to back me up when I have to discipline. There isn't someone here who I can bounce things off of when I have to decide if she can talk to boys.

These are reasons why the other truths in this book are so important. Let's recap:

- Truth #1 reminds us that even though we are the only parent in the home, '**We are not alone.**'
- Truth #2 reminds us that God's got this because '**He loves our child(ren).**'
- Truth #3 gives us those people to bounce things off of and to back us up because we have '**Community.**'
- Truth #4 reminds us to give ourselves and our children '**Grace, Grace, Grace.**'

These other truths help us whenever anything in life comes our way. There is one final truth I want to share that took me a while to learn but is so important. Truth #5 is about the importance of self and soul-care.

Let's keep it real here and say that while we take care of everyone else, we probably do not have a lot left over to take care of ourselves. If you do well in this area, I am excited for you, and I have a challenge for you. Find another single Mom that you know that maybe is not doing so well with this truth, and help her. Show her the importance of self and soul-care. Maybe give her a copy of this book (wink, wink).

If you do not do well with this truth, it's okay. That's why I'm writing this book...to help show you the importance of taking care of yourself. Not that I get it right all the time...since it's currently 1:49am and I'm up writing, when I should be asleep. So now I know I am going to be tired tomorrow, and maybe not as patient as I should or could be with my girls.

Jesus is our ultimate example. We are supposed to try and live like Him. In Luke 6:12, we get a glimpse of how Jesus took care of Himself:

> *"One of those days Jesus went out to a mountainside*
> *to pray, and spent the night praying to God."*

He spent the night praying to God. Wow. Then again in Matthew 14:23 the Bible tells us,

> *"After He had sent them away,*
> *He went up on the mountain by Himself to pray.*
> *When evening came, He was there alone."*

Jesus took time out of His days to spend them in prayer to God. I would love to say that I am doing great with soul-care right now, but there is definitely room for improvement. What about you? How is your soul-care?

I think we also have to consider other things in life, in addition to spending time with God, in order to take care of ourselves. We have to be able to fill our cup back up, so that we have more to give others. You can't pour from an empty cup. How full is your cup?

Okay so you might be sitting there thinking I am crazy, and how are you going to fit one more thing into your schedule. I don't blame you if you are feeling that way. I totally understand. But a better question is, how can you not?

I have learned, from lots of experience, that I am more equipped to handle things life throws my way when I am recharged. I think most of us can say we have some triggers that cause us to not be at our best. Can anyone say 'hangry?" Maybe it's being hungry, tired, stressed, etc.

For me, being tired or having a headache are the biggest triggers that keep me from being at my best with my girls. There have been times when I was super crabby and Andrea would ask me if I had a headache. I guess it's pretty bad if even my kids know my triggers....or maybe it's not. Maybe them recognizing it in me will help them realize in the future how important it is to take care of themselves.

I have been avoiding one thing that comes up for me a lot when I have to take care of myself and my soul...guilt. Any time I spend on myself means I am not spending time with my children. What if they think I don't love them if I'm not there? This money could really be used to get them something they need. Am I being selfish?

I've been there...and I am still a visitor to guilt at times. But let's see what the Bible has to say about taking care of ourselves:

> *Or do you not know that your body is a temple of the Holy Spirit within you, whom you have from God? You are not your own, for you were bought with a price. So glorify God in your body.*
> *1 Corinthians 6:19-20*

Well, I'm not one to argue with the Word of God...are you? It very clearly tells us to take care of our bodies. This means eating, sleeping, living. God wants us to have a full life (John 10:10), and I believe this includes things that bring us joy.

Another way we must take care of ourselves is our heart. The Bible talks about the importance of this. Luke 6:45 tells us:

> *A good man brings good things out of the good stored up in his heart, and an evil man brings evil things out of the evil stored up in his heart. For the mouth speaks what the heart is full of.*

I know for me, if my heart is full of junk like jealousy, anger, or bitterness, the words that come out of my mouth will not be very nice words. I'm sure my Mom would want to wash my mouth out with soap if she heard me talking during these moments. Lucky for me, God gave me (and you) His Word to fill our hearts with. When we are intentional, and in relationship with God on a regular basis, our hearts overflow with Him and His Word, and then OUR words are much sweeter.

I know it might be difficult to accept that we must take care of ourselves if we are going to be at our best to take care of others. I had a difficult time overcoming the "am I being selfish" question. Honestly, I still do at times. I have come to realize though, that if God wants me, and you, to take care of ourselves, how can I be selfish if I am trying to be like Him, because He is certainly not selfish.

The importance of self and soul-care

Truth #5

Go-to verses

Matthew 11:28: "Come to me, all you who are weary and burdened, and I will give you rest."

Luke 6:12: "One of those days Jesus went out to a mountainside to pray, and spent the night praying to God."

1 Corinthians 6:19-20: "Or do you not know that your body is a temple of the Holy Spirit within you, whom you have from God? You are not your own, for you were bought with a price. So glorify God in your body."

How to live it out

Applying Truth #5

Chapter Ten

I am going to start off by saying that this might be really difficult at first, but I promise you it is worth it. I'm not saying you should go on a girl's night out every night of the week or anything like that. Just find something that works for you.

That is the thing with the life application parts of these truths...you customize them to whatever fits for you. We are all in different seasons as single-moms, and what works for me might not work for you. You have to find your own ways for self and soul-care. These five tips will help you get started in living out Truth #5: The importance of self and soul-care. So let's dig in:

Tip #1 ~ Make a list

What makes you feel recharged? Maybe you have an answer right off the bat, or maybe it has been so long that you recharged that you do not have a clue. Either way, make a list. Sit down and think about things you love to do that make you happy.

Maybe you have a hobby that relaxes you. Maybe running helps you relieve stress. Start jotting down ideas and things that pop into your mind. Pray and ask God to reveal to you what might be good things to write on your list.

Tip #2 ~ Look at your calendar

There are so many things on your to-do list, and you have no idea where you would fit in time for yourself. So....go to the source. Go to your calendar right now and see where you would be able to fit in time for you.

It does not have to be an entire day, because let's be honest...who has an entire day? If you do, YAY!! But most of us won't have that kind of time. So again, this has to be what works for you. So check your calendar and see what you can do.

Tip #3 ~ Enlist help

Remember that community we talked about with Truth #3? Now would be the perfect time to enlist their help. Maybe in your list you made, coffee with a friend was on there. So reach out to that friend and ask them to get together.

Maybe in your calendar search you found a doable time, but need someone to stay with the kids. So call up someone in your community you are building and ask them for help. Maybe you can both swap childcare: she watches yours and then when she needs it, you watch hers. So instead of paying, you are both helping each other out. This is another reason community is so important for us single Moms.

Tip #4 ~ Take one step

Just one step. Even it if means taking a walk around the yard. Sitting in your car for five extra minutes in the daycare parking lot. Just do something for YOU.

You do not need to do something that takes a lot of time to care for yourself. Maybe it's soaking in a bubble bath after the kids are asleep. Having a long overdue chat with your best friend. Taking the first step is the hardest, but it is the most important because it will take you down a path that God wants for you...to take care of your body and your soul.

Tip #5 ~ Reflect

What did you do? How did it feel? Anytime we make big changes or try to make lifestyle changes, I think it is important to sit back and reflect on them. If it didn't work and we don't reflect on why, I believe there is a greater chance we will walk away and abandon this new thing.

On the other hand, if we reflect on both the good and the bad to figure out how we could do it better, then I believe we have a better chance of sticking with it. We have to know we are not going to do it perfectly, and we still might feel the guilt. But we can't allow the enemy to rob us of being the best Moms we can be, and giving our kids the best Moms they could have. Taking care of ourselves and our souls is a vital piece of this.

Taking care of ourselves is so important to taking care of our families. Are you really at your best if you're tired and snappy? I know I'm not. Or if you're stretched so thin you might snap? This does not seem like we would be giving our best to anyone, especially not God or our families.

This is a process, especially if you have not done much for yourself in your life as a single-mom. You most likely won't make huge, drastic changes overnight. It will take time. It will take perseverance. It will take grace (Truth #4). But if you stick with it, I promise you will not regret it. You will be recharged and refreshed, and ready to take on this crazy single-mom life.

Life Application Check-Up

Truth #5: The importance of self and soul-care

Truth check-ups are questions to get you thinking about how you are applying these truths to your life. Be as honest as you can and as always, there is NO JUDGEMENT. I promise.

1. What is one thing you can do to take care of yourself today?

2. If you are not sure what you can do for yourself, what is one step you can take?

3. What was your biggest takeaway from this chapter?

Final Thoughts

Life is hard. It's messy. It downright stinks a lot of days. But God. God has given us His Word to help us every step of the way. He has given me these life lessons to help along the way...and to share them with you.

My prayer is that you will be able to reflect on and apply these five truths to your life. There is no one-size-fits-all way to apply them. Do what works best for you, your season of life, and your family.

I still don't always get it right, and I know there will always be times I do not get it right. And that's okay. I'm a work in progress and God is not finished with me yet. He's not finished with you yet either.

Made in the USA
Columbia, SC
27 January 2018